Smart Investing In:

TABLE OF CONTENT

INTRODUCTION

Congratulations on downloading this book and thank you for doing so!

We can now look back on five years as an investor in the global real estate market. The portfolio is now worth 180 billion kroner and consists of properties of a high standard in key markets in the US and Europe.

Since inception in 2011, unlisted real estate investments have returned 6.9 percent. Returns in unlisted markets in a single year should not be given too much weight. We are still in an early phase, but each year that passes gives us a better indication of the contribution real estate investments makes to the fund.

There has been increased uncertainty in financial markets recently, but this has not had a major impact on the unlisted real estate to date. Yields in most markets are record-low. Even record-high real estate prices are producing strong excess returns over fixed-income investments. Most letting markets are also relatively solid, with good rents and low vacancy. We nevertheless believe that the current uncertainty could result in weaker results ahead. However, the fund has a very long investment horizon and a substantial capacity to absorb and exploit short-term fluctuations.

We invest when we see good opportunities in line with our strategy, and we hold back when the risks outweigh the expected returns.

Our organisation has grown with our investments and now includes employees at six offices in five time zones. To ensure capacity, specialist expertise and an organisation and investment

culture tailored to investments in the unlisted market, the real estate operation were reorganised as a separate unit in 2014. We are working actively to establish the necessary infrastructure to ensure sound management of an ever-growing portfolio of unlisted real estate investments.

Openness about our activities is important, and less information is publicly available in the unlisted market. Our aim with this report is to explain how we go about investing in unlisted real estate and how these investments are managed.

Our mission is to safeguard and build financial wealth for future generations. The goal for our investments, therefore, is to generate a good long-term return with acceptable risk, responsibly and transparently.

INVESTING IN REAL ESTATE

Real estate is a popular investment. There are many modifications in the monetary system having a puffed-up risk or lesser returns, the investment marketplace goes on with the plan imaginative and good-looking investment approaches. These developments make it important for real estate licenses to have an elementary and up-to-date knowledge of real estate investment. Of course, this does not mean that licenses should act as investment counselors. For all the time they should refer investors to knowledgeable tax accountants, attorneys, or investment professionals. These are the professionals who can give expert advice on an investor's specific needs.

Consider All the Three Factors Before Investing in Real Estate

The three factors of investing in real estate are area, perception, and economics. The key to making the best investment in real estate, and specifically in cooperatives, and townhouses, is to consider all the three factors. Investing in real estate correspond to certain commitments on the part of the purchaser. Investment in real estate made solely upon the location of the property will not yield those results. Before making an investment, it is essential to include the three considerations

 Consider on the whole area.

 Consider awareness of the area.

 Consider the financial factors.

Merits of Real Estate Investment:

Real estate values have varied extensively in various areas of the country. Yet many real estate investments have shown above average rates of return, generally greater than the prevailing interest rates charged by mortgage lenders. In assumption, this means the investor can utilize the influence of rented money to invest a real estate purchase and feel comparatively sure that, if held long enough, the asset will yield more money than it cost to finance the purchase.

Real estate offers investors greater control over their investments than do other options such as stocks etc. Real estate investors also are given assured tax advantages.

Demerits of Real Estate Investment:

Liquidity refers to how quickly an asset may be converted into cash. For instance, an investor in listed stocks has only a call a stockbroker when funds are needed. The stockbroker sells the stock, and the investor receives the cash. In contract, a real estate investor may have to sell the property at a substantially lower price than desired to ensure a quick sale. Of course, a real estate investor may be able to raise a limited amount of cash by refinancing the property.

Huge amounts are generally necessary to invest in real estate. It is not easy to invest in real estate without professional guidance. Investment decisions must be based on careful studies of all the facts, reinforced by a thorough knowledge of real estate and the manner in which it is affected by the marketplace.

Real estate has need of dynamic administration. A real estate investor can rarely sit idly by and watch his or her money grow. Administration assessments must be made. The investor may want to manage the property personally. On the other hand, it may be preferable to hire a professional property manager. Physical improvements accomplished by the investor personally may be required to make the asset profitable. Many good investments fail because of poor management.

Finally, it involves a high degree of risk. The opportunity forever survives that an investor's property will diminish in rate during the time it is held or that it will not make enough income to make it advantageous.

WHAT YOU NEED TO KNOW ABOUT REAL ESTATE INVESTING

Are you interested in making a living as a real estate investor? If you are, your career and your financial future will rely heavily on your real estate investing skills, knowledge, and actions. If you have yet to quit your current job, to enter into real estate investing, you will want to continue reading on before doing so.

When it comes to real estate investing, there are many hopeful investors who think that it is easy to make money as a real estate investor. Yes, it can be easy, but it isn't always. Real estate investing is a risky business. Real estate markets, all across the country regularly change; therefore, you aren't given any guarantees. That is why it may be a good idea to start out small, by only purchasing one or two real estate properties first. This will give you the opportunity to determine if you can be successful with real estate investing and without having to go broke finding out that you can't.

Although real estate investing is considered a risky business, there are steps that you can take to improve your chances of making money with it. Perhaps, the most important thing that you can do is educate yourself about real estate investing. Be sure to focus on more than just real estate investing in general. Be sure to learn about foreclosure properties, fixer upper properties, becoming a landlord, and such. Unfortunately, too many hopeful investors mistakenly believe that real estate investing simply involves buying real estate, but it is more than that. To be a successful real estate investor, this is a fact that you must not forget.

When it comes to familiarizing yourself with the many components of real estate investing, you will see that you have a number of different options. For instance, there are a number of online websites that aim to provide internet users to free information on real estate investing. There are also printed resource guides or real estate investing books that can be purchased. For more detailed information with a professional spin, you can take a real estate investment training course or class, many of which are held by successful real estate investors.

As it was previously mentioned, to make a successful career out of real estate investing, you need to be able to do more than just buy and sell properties. When it comes to real estate investment properties many properties are repaired or updated and then rented out. Most commonly the landlord in charge of making all decisions is the property owner or the investor, which could be you. For you to make money in that aspect, you would need to make sure that all of your houses or apartments were filled with tenants. Do you know how you would go about doing so? Better yet, do you think that you could do so? If not, real estate investing may not be right for you.

The above-mentioned points are points that you will want to take into consideration before quitting your current job and banking on the real estate market. Yes, real estate investing is a great way to make money, but it isn't for everyone. Your first step should involve determining whether or not it is right for you.

COMMERCIAL REAL ESTATE INVESTING - WHAT YOU NEED TO KNOW

Commercial Real Estate Investing Basics

Commercial real estate investing is a terrific way to make money if you know how to invest correctly. Commercial investing means that you are making real estate transactions that don't apply to single-family homes. Instead, you are investing in apartment complexes, retail properties, office buildings, educational buildings, warehouses, manufacturing facilities, etc.

There are several real estate properties that are deemed as commercial. This may even be a vacant lot were a future commercial building could be structured. Even parking lots could be considered a commercial investment. Or there is already a working business on the lot of lands that you are investing in.

When you choose to get involved in commercial real estate investing, you are putting your money in a reasonably safe place. And more than likely, you will have some great returns if you are smart about your investments. This type of investing has a lot of potential for making the big bucks.

For you, for you to do well in commercial investing, you will want to educate yourself. You can do this by attending investment seminars or courses, or even reading some do-it-yourself literature. You will want to know everything you can about what you are doing with your hard-earned money.

Why Commercial Real Estate

Commercial real estate investing is really attractive because it lets investors build equity, supply rental income, and just earn money to use for your own business. Depending on what you want to do and the type of money you want to get back, there are several procedures in managing your investments and properties. You may want to consider taking more than just a few informal courses if you are serious about investing in commercial real estate. You might want to think about taking some specific classes on commercial investing.

Buying property instead of renting it will permit you to gain equity. When you own the property, you can also manage it how you want and won't have to worry about the rules and stipulations put on you by an owner other than you.

If you are playing with the idea of commercial real estate investing you will want to do some research, educate yourself, make lists of your goals and how you can achieve them, and compare the advantages and disadvantages to help you make decisions. When you follow these steps, making the right decisions will be an easier process for you.

ALL ABOUT REAL ESTATE AGENTS

Real estate agents are professionals instrumental in connecting the buyer with the seller.

Additionally, many real estate agents manage rentals wherein they introduce tenants to landlords and oversee the maintenance of the property on behalf of the landlords.

In most areas, real estate agents are required to be highly educated, licensed and are regulated by a governing body.

Some real estate agents are also Realtors.

To use the title Realtor, a real estate agent must be a member of the National Association of Realtors which in addition to a number of other requirements, requires Realtors to adhere to a strict code of ethics and offers Realtors additional educational and designation opportunities.

Though not required by rule or law, it might be a wise decision to seek the services of a Realtor.

What Do They Do?

Real estate agents bring together two or more interested parties, perform those steps necessary to successfully conclude a transaction and charge a commission for their services.

For sales transactions, they charge commission to the seller while for rentals, the commission is typically charged the landlord.

Real estate agents generally calculate their fee as a percentage of the selling price (in the case of a sale) and as part of the rent for rental units.

How Do They Do It?

People who want to sell or rent their property leave details of their property with the real estate agent.

Along with all property details the real estate agent will typically have keys to the house to facilitate showings.

The other interested party (i.e. the buyer/tenant), gets access to this information and to the property by contacting the real estate agent.

That's how the real estate agent becomes a hub of information.

Contrary to some common misconceptions, real estate agents typically represent the seller or the buyer but rarely both.

Why Should I Use One..

First and foremost, to protect yourself. Real estate transactions are highly regulated, highly paper (document) intensive transactions.

The real estate agent possesses an in-depth knowledge of the laws, rules, regulations, disclosures and documentation necessary to successfully complete the transaction to the satisfaction of the buyer, the seller and the law.

Because real estate agents are most familiar with local real estate market conditions, it is wise and makes sense to seek the advice of one to get an idea of the current trends and pricing for properties within that market.

A good real estate agent will know the prices (or price range) of various properties of different types and at various locations within the region.

Because of the real estate agent's knowledge and expertise, property sellers often get a few thousand dollars more for their property.

Many home seekers, including seasoned real estate investors use the services of real estate agents to locate the best real estate bargains in the easiest and quickest manner.

Furthermore, the best agents analyze the wants and needs of a home buyer/tenant and provide valuable input as to the kinds of properties available to them within their budget. Therefore, a good real estate agent will not just present a list of available properties to the buyer/tenant but will actually discuss their needs and make suggestions.

The good real estate agent, working in this manner benefits in at least two ways.

First and most obviously, when the real estate agent is able to successfully complete the transaction the commission is earned and the real estate agent is paid...

and secondly, if they make the customer/client happy they earn a good reputation and often receive referrals (hence more business).

Worth Noting.

It is worth noting that there is a myth floating around that real estate agents only work on behalf of the seller, buyer beware.

This is not written in stone nor is it always the case. Real estate agents are, in most regions, highly regulated.

With few exceptions, real estate agents work either for the seller (as is the case with many listing agents) or for the buyer (as is the case for a buyer's agent).

Additionally, some areas allow for dual agency where an agent can work for both the seller and the buyer or as a transaction broker where the agent represents the transaction itself and neither the seller nor buyer individually.

However, in the case of dual agency/transaction brokerage, note that rule, regulation (law) and ethics do not permit the agent to act in favor of either party while in detriment to the other.

If you are unsure of the relationship between you and your real estate agent, do not hesitate to ask.

ALL ABOUT REAL ESTATE BRIDGE LOANS

In today's times, buying a home is no longer considered as an extraordinary thing to do. These days there are numerous financing options available in the market than ever before. The home buyer can now opt for loans, be it conventional loan or adjustable rate types. With so much variety of choices available, a home buyer can definitely find a suitable loan for himself. While looking for a loan, a home buyer should keep his current financial situation as well as future plans, in mind. Many people dream of buying a house but only few of them can really achieve this goal. These days, many people want to buy real estate property but buying it entirely by cash is not practically possible to most of them by taking help of a real estate loan, their dream of purchasing a home can come true. With the real estate loan, one can easily plan and own a property for himself.

People opt for these with various intentions. Some may want to invest in the real estate market by buying a corporative flat, others would like to reconstruct their existing real estate and some may plan to build a property. Various types of loans are easily available in order to fulfill their needs accordingly. One can easily come across many financing agencies such as banks and money lending forms who offer real estate loans to people. Since the money involved is much higher than the ordinary loans, there are certain prerequisites to obtain the loan.

Real estate loans can be categorized as a secured loan since the borrower needs to handle over a legal document to his lender. By this way, the borrower and the owner of the new property transfers the collateral to the lender which acts as security against the offered loan amount. This produce is adapted since the lender is lending big money. Hence the lender wants his money to be secured and wants a sort of a guarantee from the borrower that it will be paid on time. It is with such kind of assurance deal that the lender accepts the loan to the borrower.

While dealing with these, one must be aware that the payback tenure or repayment period is another important factor while deciding on a real estate loan plan. One must also be aware of the fact that the longer the repayment tenure, the lower will be the installments and thus the borrower finds it easy to payback. There are two types of real estate loans. They are as follows:

• Residential Loans: Before a person applies for the loan, he has to follow certain pre-requisites. Firstly, a residential loan online application form has to be filled. Secondly, his last financial statement and his latest income tax return documents have to be furnished. He must also be in a position to submit one guarantor's most recent individual financial statement and latest individual tax return.

• Commercial Loan: The prerequisites before applying for the commercial real estate loan are as follows:

1. The commercial real estate online application loan online application form has to be filled up followed by the real estate appendix

2. The present company's financial statements and latest tax return needs to be furnished

3. Finally, guarantor's most recent individual financial statement and latest individual tax return has to be handed over.

ALL ABOUT REAL ESTATE DEVELOPERS

Real estate developers in Spain are a vital part of the country's real estate industry. When real estate is booming the developers do really well because the demand for the homes has increased. When the real estate is not under demand, the developers may not get as much business then they are accustomed to. Even though this is not an ideal situation, most experienced Spanish developers know how to handle the market so they can always make a profit.

What is a real estate Developer?

A property developer is someone, either a company or an individual, who makes it their business to handle the development, including the building of, real estate. Development companies range from small to very large. The larger development projects, for example, will likely go to a larger firm - maybe one that specializes in commercial development. If there is property for sale in Spain chances are there was someone who developed it. These companies stand to make a large profit depending on how well the market is doing.

Why Spanish real estate?

Spanish real estate development has seen an increase in recent years because Spain has become a desirable location. As a result, the property market has risen steadily. This means that the developers have had a lot of work to do and they've been making a nice profit. However, they have experienced a slowdown. It is likely that the companies will go elsewhere for their development such as Latin America.

Should you contact a developer?

When you set out to buy Spanish real estate you will either be faced with the opportunity to buy the property right from the developer or from the existing owner. If you want something that is new or something that you will design yourself, you will need to get in contact with a Spanish developer.

If you purchase the land yourself, you will need to find a way to get something builds on it. This is where developers come in handy. You can find a good developer for your Spanish real estate project by looking online or asking around. There may be a developer whose work you admire. Or you may just want someone reliable. Whatever your needs are, there is a developer that will fit them.

What kind of developer?

There are different kinds of developers out there. Some specialize in commercial properties, others in residential properties or apartments. Developers all have something that they are best at. If you are serious about finding the right developer, these are factors you need to keep in mind. Just remember that Real estate developers in Spain are a vital part of the housing market and something that can greatly benefit you while searching for property.

ALL ABOUT REAL ESTATE INVESTMENT OPPORTUNITIES

If you were to believe all that you hear on the news in recent months, you can be left believing that the entire real estate market in the U.S. is on a steady downhill slide. However; the fact themselves can be deceiving, because what is most often being presented on the national news, is national averages that doesn't give consideration to individual regions, such as the Bellaire real estate market in Houston Texas.

New Revitalization Programs,

New revitalization efforts in several areas of Houston, including Bellaire, has led to a stabilization and in many instances measurable appreciation in home values. This has left the door wide open to savvy real estate investors, who are once aging looking to get back into the lucrative business of real estate investing.

Back to Basics,

Buying and flipping fixer-uppers are once again looking practical and profitable, however, there are a few things that you have to bear in mind. Towards the end of the last real estate boom, the term "fixer-upper" was completely forgotten about, as people found that they could turn a handy profit on a home without ever having to touch the investment property that they had purchased.

Estimating Repairs,

While this is once again possible in most instances it is simply not the case. This means that just like ten years ago, it is imperative that you be able to estimate costs on renovations and actually do profitable repairs and renovations if you plan on succeeding in today's tighter real estate market.

Learn to Estimate Home Repairs ,

This doesn't necessarily mean that you have to be an expert in home repairs. However; it sure helps if you know how to recognize and estimate repairs on crucial areas of a home such as foundations and roofs. Also, you may want to get some painting equipment together and learn to use it, because a good paint job is the most cost-effective and immediate way to increase to looks and value of a distressed home or commercial property.

ALL ABOUT REAL ESTATE MOBILE MARKETING

Real estate properties and investments form a very significant part of every country's economy regardless of where a country may be located. Property investment actually deals with the problem of congestion and housing in almost every city in the world. For this area to fully develop, a lot is required in terms of market research and creating awareness to consumers of this service. This has revolutionized the nature of advertising, hence leading to real estate mobile marketing.

One of the easiest ways to handle any transaction in the current world is by the use of a mobile phone. Advertising services through cell phones have gained prominence because almost all individuals above 18 years of age have a phone. The use of this device for advertising can help business sales make a huge turn-around.

A property investor just needs to find an expert in the market analysis of properties. These experts could be single individuals or advertising and property firms. The investor will then provide all the details concerning the property such as the location, the description, what it can be used for, the cost and the terms and conditions involved in the acquisition of such an investment.

These experts then design the advertisements in a manner that is appealing and attractive. The categories of these adverts may include those phones that support pictures, videos and those that don't support. The message is as brief as possible but straight to the point. It provides the reader with a great deal of information that is necessary.

Due to the growth of this sector, there are now several companies that are fully dedicated to providing these services. With the competition for customers, they now offer services at relatively affordable prices. The result in the long run is a lot of sales and profit.

The issue of real estate mobile marketing is very simple. The investor just needs to get the identification numbers of the properties that they sell. It is this number that is available. When they need more information about that particular kind of property, then they will get it instantly via phone text messages. The text message content can be changed as frequently as needed. Signs may then be placed with the identity numbers of the listed property as feedback is awaited.

When a buyer wishes to purchase an investment of your choice, they will view a sign at the property and the mobile number of the assigned agent attached to the said property put in the market. In case they want more information on this kind of investment, they will call the agent using the displayed number. These advertising agents are usually available 24/7. This solves the whole problem of marketing as information is now delivered efficiently.

Real estate mobile marketing is actually one of the advertising features that have changed the whole marketing approach of this profusely growing industry. The property market has seen the sales of properties multiply over a few years. This is actually why all investors need to give it a try and be sure of results

ALL ABOUT REAL ESTATE AND HOMES IN MOORESVILLE

While real estate markets in just about every area of the U.S. continue to decline and are projected to do so at least into the near future, the greater Charlotte NC area including Mooresville continues to prosper. This means that now is the time to find the Mooresville NC home for sale you are looking for because growth and profits in real estate are projected to continue on unaffected by the recession that is plaguing the rest of the U.S.

The fact is, that Mooresville is a bedroom community for Charlotte NC and as long as Charlotte continues on its path of prosperity, so too goes its surrounding communities including Mooresville. The business climate of Mooresville is unusual in that it is home to more than 60 NASCAR racing teams and the surrounding businesses that support those 60 teams.

It is also home to the headquarters of the Lowe's Hardware chain, so the Mooresville economy is fueled by businesses that aren't susceptible to economic fluctuations. This is just one of the many factors that have all contributed to Mooresville and the greater Charlotte NC areas 6% increase in real estate values in 2008.

The home building industry is still active and viable in the greater Charlotte area due to its steady, consistent growth and this means that finding a Mooresville NC home for sale in your price range is just as easy as it was, say, four years ago. Also, the simple fact of the matter is that Mooresville is a great place to live and raise a family due to the fact that they just don't have a lot of the big city problems that so many other areas tend to be plagued with. Also with the median price range on a home in the greater Charlotte NC area presently at $225,000 you will find prices far more affordable on any sized home when compared to other similar market areas.

THINK REAL ESTATE INVESTING IS ALL ABOUT REAL ESTATE?

Someone once said real estate investing is all about the money. Were they right? Well, let's face it, the bottom line when it comes to this business, and every other business is money. Money doesn't just make the world go 'round, it also clarifies our thinking as we try to fit the pieces of the property investing game together.

There is a side to the property flipping business that is rarely discussed, and that's the money-lending side. Whether you're talking to a conventional bank to get your financing ducks lined up, or a private lender, you should understand how the financing game works. You might even find it's what you'd rather do instead of flipping houses.

Lending money is a great way to make money flipping houses

It turns out there are a lot of folks making good money by providing private lending services to property investors. The fact is, you can make just as much money and in many cases a lot more, by acting as a bank for other investors.

The 6 Secrets of Lending That Bankers Don't Want You to Know

1. Banker's vertical stacking strategy. This is simply a way to leverage money to increase your yield beyond a simple interest rate return on investment. There are several lending techniques that, when stacked together, multiply your yield.

2. Shifting the risk. This is a game all banks play with borrowers. The idea is to shift the risk. Lending is all about safety, so it's important to shift the risk to the borrower.

3. Shifting the work. As a lender, we want to make as much money as possible with as little risk as possible and have as much free time as possible. What could possibly be wrong with that?

4. It's a financing game. When you invest in properties you have a physical asset like a rental home that pays about 10%, and you've got a mortgage and other expenses that amount to about 7%, so you end up with a 3% spread. When you're the lender you have no physical asset like a rental property and none of the accompanying headaches like evictions or damaged property to deal with. Being a private lender is the most efficient way to generate passive income and continuous cash flow.

5. The ultimate secret. The ultimate lending secret really consists of several components:

• You can become a private lender without using any of your own money.

• You can do it without having any credit, and without ever having your credit checked.

• Anyone can do this.

6. Re-Hypothecation is the most powerful word in banking. When a borrower signs on a piece of paper, called a mortgage, that piece of paper can be used as collateral for a loan.

Now that you know about the other side of real estate investing, the lending side, perhaps you should consider it as an alternative. Not worrying about physical assets, bad tenants and repairing damaged property can be a blessing. It's something to think about as you make your mark and build your business.

LEARN ABOUT REAL ESTATE INVESTING - ONLINE GUIDES TO REAL ESTATE INVESTING

What is there to learn about real estate investing that hasn't already been learned? Are there any new methods or techniques out there that can give someone a sharper edge in this field? Well yes, actually... there are new methods and old techniques, but these aren't part of the usual subject matter of most training courses today.

Most of these techniques and methods are only learned by grueling experiences of trial and error, and usually only shared amongst certain circles. They aren't exceedingly secretive circles - you obviously wouldn't have to be a Freemason or anything like that in order to learn them. But the simple fact is that the best techniques to learn about real estate investing are just not taught in common courses. You would have to learn them from an experienced mentor.

There are some such people who teach others through online means. It is from these people that you can find out all the most effective strategies there are to learn about real estate investing today. There are methods to use in investing that require no involvement with credit in any way, and techniques of investing using no loans or involvement with any banks whatsoever - these are the things to learn about real estate investing that can change your career.

After all, if you can invest little and then profit big, and all without involving anything to do with credit or banks, then that would be the proverbial "philosopher's stone" of real estate investing, right? Find an online mentor and learn about real estate investing today.

HOW TO LEARN ABOUT REAL ESTATE - REAL ESTATE INVESTMENT

The trick to how to learn about real estate, for beginners, is really no trick at all. There are classes and courses to take to earn your certificates and licenses and be armed with enough knowledge to begin a bright and prosperous career in this industry. However, we may discover that those who have been in this field for years, and who have gained the know-how from such long experience in this business, things seem to go rather swimmingly.

It appears that all of the accomplishments we undertake for them seem to be done with so much more simplicity, taking less time, and reaping higher profits. They also seem to know full well just what pitfalls to avoid. If only we knew how to learn all that they have learned about in real estate from the get go, then we could prosper just as much even from our meager beginnings.

Mentoring is the answer here, finding in such a person all we need to know is how to learn about this field. Real estate can be tricky, and we need to be able to benefit from the knowledge of these seasoned veterans. The only problem is in finding someone who is willing to divulge all of their inside techniques to one of us greenhorns who desperately need it the most. This is why it is best to learn such things online. Using the internet is how to learn about all we need to know in real estate as far as higher learning goes. In this distance-learning method, we can find someone willing to guide us in this field without it affecting their personal corner of the real estate world.

THE NAKED TRUTH ABOUT REAL ESTATE INVESTING

I promise to give you the absolute truth about real estate investing, or better yet, what we all know as 'flipping homes' and then from there you figure out if wholesaling homes for a living is a scam or do you really have it in you to be a wholesaler.

Flipping homes from what I see has become completely blown out of proportion. Many people are looking at this as a get rich quick thing where they think you read a few eBooks, print out some papers, draw up some bandit signs and build this massive never ending list of cash buyers.

Well, that is what it's about trust and believe it's NOT easy....in the beginning.

Just like anything in life you have to get your name out there. Get people talking about you. Good talk hopefully but it's just like when you go out for a job interview.

You want to leave a lasting impression so that you get that call back.

Well, you want to have cash buyers blowing your phone off the hook but the actual truth about real estate investing is they aren't going to unless they...

1. Know who you are or.....

2. You have an amazing deal

Once you bring amazing wholesale deals to the table, they will want to work with you and that's how you build a list of repeat buyers.It's all about investing and you have to invest 1 of 2 things and if you have both, it won't take much for you to be successful in real estate investing.

1. You need to have money to invest (money talks; no money then talk is cheap unless...

2. you bring expertise to the table

It's deeper than learning how to fill out contracts or how to go to the title office without GPS and pick up a check.

The absolute truth about real estate investing: To be a great wholesaler, you must give out true and accurate figures, otherwise you make a bad name for yourself.

To be able to cook in the kitchen of flipping houses, you need these 3 main ingredients:

1. The ability to contract RE at great discounts through negotiation tactics.

2. The ability to build a real cash buyer list (larger, the better)

3. Ability to evaluate your market and ability to give close estimated rehab numbers. Both of these require a vast knowledge of the local market conditions and the know-how to quote repair items.

Without ALL 3 of these items, you CAN NOT be a true wholesaler.

To add a 4th item, you should be honest, provide accurate numbers, and provide as much due diligence to your potential buyers as possible.

This will allow you to keep your buyers coming back for more deals.

WHAT DO THE EXPERTS SAY ABOUT REAL ESTATE INVESTING FOR BEGINNERS?

If you're looking for new ways to make a living or just a few bucks on the side, maybe you should consider real estate investing for beginners. Many people are intimidated by the thought of jumping into something new. The thinking usually follows along these lines:

There's too much to learn...

Startup costs are too high...

There's nobody to turn to for help...

It goes on and on. There are no shortages of excuses for not starting a new venture. While they all sound reasonable, these excuses serve no purpose other than to prevent you from taking action.

It's not as scary as you think.

The truth is, real estate investing for beginners is not a scary monster. In fact, it's just the opposite. It's an easy, affordable and very profitable way to make money. By taking the advice of the pros who have gone before you and learning from their mistakes, you can learn to make the same kind of serious money they're making, and without enduring the painful learning curve they had to suffer through.

A few methods the pros use to make serious money in real estate:

• Flipping Homes - This is an excellent way to get started. Once you've established a relationship with a real estate professional, you'll learn how you can flip homes without using any of your own money. You can establish that relationship by taking one of the top online courses out there. The best ones will show you how to finance your homes using private money lenders. It's easier than you think.

• HUD Wholesaling of Homes - This is actually just a variation on the house flipping process. The best HUD house wholesaling professionals use a special system for offering, buying and then selling HUD properties. You can learn the system via easy online flipping and wholesaling courses.

• Owning Rental Properties - Buying and holding onto rental properties is a great way to make good money on an ongoing basis. Nothing beats regular fixed income from rentals, month after month, year after year. Once again, the best online courses will show you how to buy, repair and rent properties by following a proven formula.

These are just a few of the more popular ways real estate investing for beginners can turn the novice into the wealthy real estate guru. Better watch out! Before you know it you'll be the expert everyone goes to for the real estate secrets for making big money.

WHAT YOU SHOULD KNOW ABOUT REAL ESTATE BUSINESS

Real estate or immovable property is a legal term (in some jurisdictions) that encompasses land along with anything permanently affixed to the land, such as buildings. Real estate (immovable property) is often considered synonymous with real property (also sometimes called realty), in contrast with personal property (also sometimes called chattel or personalty).

In British usage, however, "real property", often shortened to just "property", refers rather to land and fixtures as such while the term "real estate" is used mostly in the context of probate law, and means all interests in land held by a deceased person at death excluding interests in money arising under a trust for sale of or charged on land.

In French, Italian and Spanish, real estate is called "immovables" (immobiliser in French, immobile in Italian and inmueble in Spanish); other property is called "movables" (mobilier and mueble).

With the development of private property ownership, real estate has become a major area of business. Within each field, a business may spccialize in a particular type of real estate. Specialists are often called on to valuate real estate and facilitate transactions. Within each field, a business may specialize in a particular type of real estates, such as residential, commercial, or industrial property.

Purchasing real estate requires a significant investment, and each parcel of land has unique characteristics, so the real estate industry has evolved into several distinct fields.

In addition, almost all construction business effectively has a connection to real estate. Banks are willing to make such loans at favorable rates in large part because, if the borrower does not make payments, the lender can foreclose by filing a court action that lets them take back the property and sell it to get their money back.

In recent years, many economists have recognized that the lack of effective real estate laws can be a significant barrier to investment in many developing countries. Real estate in Mexico and Central America is not the same in many ways as it is in the United States. Some similarities are that there are legal hoops to jump through and people you need to pay to help you do this (usually lawyers and real estate agents), there will be taxes (less than in the United States), there are papers to check out to make sure the owner really owns the property (again, lawyers can help you with the title search), and if you do it right, there will be a neutral party to hold the title and the money and make the switch.

I hope that everyone, from the aspiring new agent to the veteran running their own brokerage, will find this information helpful to them in bringing about real estate success.

THE TRUTH ABOUT REAL ESTATE FINANCING

One of the first steps, before you start looking for your dream house, is to ask yourself what you can afford to spend on a monthly house payment. Keep in mind when financing real estate that the lenders will be able to tell you only what you **MIGHT** be able to afford based on your salary and level of debt including any credit card debt. As the real estate market continues to grow and new technology gains ground, widely accepted beliefs that were true just a few years ago may not be true today.

You want to work with your mortgage broker or lender to develop an individual loan or mortgage program based on your credit worthiness. Your property taxes may be deductible. Consult with your CPA or other tax advisor for current tax information. With an adjustable rate mortgage, the initial interest rate is usually lower than with a fixed-rate mortgage and the monthly payment will also be lower.

If you're on a fixed income, an adjustable rate mortgage (ARM), especially a short-term ARM, may not be your best choice. And some lenders may impose limits on how much of your down payment can come from borrowing from other sources. Real estate financing is unique for each buyer.

If you're buying a second home or second property, you'll need to identify the sources for your down payment, since you'll not be selling your current house and using the proceeds. Expect a larger monthly payment for housing or other expenses too. Most adjustable rate mortgage programs do offer "rate cap" protection, which limits the amount the rate can be increased - each year and over the life of the loan. All adjustable rate mortgages are amortized over 30 years. Check with your CPA or accounting professional - you may be able to deduct the interest you pay on the mortgage loan and some of the financing costs of the home, like the points on your income tax return.

If you're having a problem getting a loan or home mortgage consider getting a lease-option on a property. A lease-option on the property will allow you to establish a good purchase price now, and then apply a portion of the rent each month toward your down payment, building equity in the process. A mortgage application can be resubmitted several times and it's not uncommon for this to happen either. I've seen it happen many times. If you have less-than-perfect or a 'bad credit' credit report don't worry too much.

If you do borrow money for a down payment it must be disclosed to the lender or if any of your money for your down payment was a gift, be ready to provide proof for it. And the interest rate for an adjustable-rate mortgage may be adjusted up or down at predetermined times; then the monthly payment will increase or decrease. The disadvantages of a fixed-rate mortgage include a possibly higher cost because these loans are usually priced higher than an adjustable rate mortgage.

Advantages of adjustable rate mortgages include: lower costs - because they're usually priced lower than fixed-rate mortgages so you can increase your buying power and lower your initial monthly payments. And if the interest rates go down, you'll have lower payments. Usually, an adjustable rate mortgage is the best choice for homeowners who are purchasing their first home and plan to be in the property for only three to five years or for those people who plan to relocate in the same period of time.

Make sure to get lots of advice about real estate financing, mortgages, interest rates, mortgage rates, mortgage refinance, bad credit mortgages, etc., and think about what makes sense to you. Thinking positive about your real estate financing is important but so is being realistic. Before you finish your real estate financing read every real estate contract and loan or home mortgage contract thoroughly before you sign on the dotted line; every line is important. Look for anything that is not specific or vague. And don't be afraid to question what you don't understand.

INFORMATION ABOUT REAL ESTATE IN GURGAON

Gurgaon, the national capital region of India, is remained the place where the scope of real estate business in highly extensive. Easy availability of quality housing at affordable prices and the quality of construction is making Gurgaon investment-worthy. In fact, Gurgaon is considered to be one of the hottest suburbs to make an investment in. The value of property in Gurgaon is likely to increase 15-20 percent annually for the next few years. This city has reshaped the realty sector of India as it has pioneered the emergence of the luxury segment during 2004-05 with the launch of DLF's Aralias; Aralias II; MGF Vilas; DLF's Magnolia and lately Ambience Caitriona and Unitech Karma Lakelands. These high-end projects provide 4-5 bedrooms, centrally air-conditioned luxury apartments with lavish specifications and all the modern facilities for customers' satisfaction.

This trend of high-class dwelling has also provided a boost to the need of purchasing in Gurgaon real estate for the purpose of functioning it as a weekend home. To satisfy the rising demand of properties, many renowned real estate developers have made initiatives for the construction of new projects which consist of both middle and high-end budget projects at MG Road, Sohna Road, Golf Course Road and Old Gurgaon Road. Out of which Sohna Road and Golf course road are seeing most of the action with new projects including The Palm Drive and The Palm Springs by Emaar MGF, Belgravia at Central park 2 and Raisina by Tata Housing coming up here.

Residential dwellings built around a golf course are the latest buzzword in the high-premium housing segment of the Indian realty industry, estimated at around $20 billion and growing at nearly 40 percent a year. Developers are making an all-out effort to create high-end apartments and villas in golf-centric communities and selling these projects by invitation only. These super-premium projects are not available cheaply with the price range starting from USD 1 million onwards.

Aside from high-priced dwellings and state-of-the-art office spaces, the city also provides a wide range of residential properties for the middle-class segment. This segment of residential apartments in Gurgaon builds the very foundation for the mass ongoing constructions. Recently, the DLF has launched "New Town Heights" and Vatika limited has come up with "Vatika India Next" for a section of society who have mid-budget for home buying. Owing to its proximity to south Delhi, the city has further enhanced its position as a world-class real estate destination for investors of India and abroad as well as the connectivity to the international airport in Delhi gives Gurgaon a vital edge over other cities in the NCR.

THE COMMON QUESTIONS AND QUERIES ABOUT REAL ESTATE TRANSACTIONS

Real estate business is not as simple as it used to be. Earlier there were just the buyer and the seller who were a part of the deal as well as the contract. Now the picture has changed considerably.

The Involved Parties,

A home buyer does not just directly walk into the property and check it before finalizing the deal with the seller. One would at least make the use of a real estate agency before finalizing the deal. These agencies get us the best property as per the requirements set forward. A professional home inspector is employed to check out the whole property. Any irregularities that need to be brought to light will be informed and documented in the real estate contracts.

The service of a financial institute may also be taken for the financing of the property. All of these need to be legally documented in the contract. The consequences in the taxing too can be a concern for certain sellers. So they may also be looking forward to get the expert services of financiers for this purpose.

The role of the real estate agents,

It is quite natural that one may wonder why to involve two agents in this whole deal regarding real estate contracts. A listing agent will bring one closer to the type of property as required. They have an important role to fulfill and they work from the buyer's point of view. The showing agent too will be on the buyer's side. But the buyer has to be cautious and wise about the decisions. The negatives of the property will not be disclosed by the agents for their own interests. That is why people hire buying agents and the commission for the property will be their fees.

Role of an attorney,

This is a relevant question and depends majorly on the situation at hand. If it is a simple deal the agents are enough but if it is a complex deal you should have your lawyer by your side. The last thing one wants to do is to sign off important rights on real estate sales agreements.

Once you sign the listing agreement for the sale, you will have to pay the commission to the listing agents. So it is wiser to always consult your friends before signing this. This enables you to exclude them from the listing agent and pay no commission if they are interested in buying.

ABOUT REAL ESTATE INVESTING - DO YOU WANT A NEW JOB?

People across the world have gained a huge amount of interest in estate investing. However, the subject of real estate and all the details involved in this business can be quite intimidating for newbies. The good news is that a new investor doesn't really have to be an expert to make it big in this industry.

Defining Estate Investment,

Investing in real properties is more than just purchasing huge tracts of land. It also includes managing, renting, and eventually selling, real properties for the intention of making a profit. Having at least a working knowledge of all these aspects is necessary to understand all there is to know about the industry.

Ways to Invest in property,

There are many ways to invest in real properties. The most basic ones are rental and sale of such properties. However, there are other means of investment such as investment groups, real estate trading, REITs, and leveraging.

The Basic Rental Investment,

Almost everyone understands how a rental investment works. This business model has been around the feudal age. The idea is that someone owns the land (or property) and people rent it and pay the needed fees.

Estate Trading,

This is the total opposite of any buy and holds business model like renting and developing. Investors who engage in trading buy properties only to own them for a short amount of time (about a few months and no more). The idea or technique here is to sell the property as soon as possible and make profitable gains in the sale, which is also known as flipping.

Estate Investment Groups,

This investment option is evidence that there is more to learn about property investing. It's pretty much like a basic rental investment but the difference is that the investors let the investment group do all the dirty work of being done by the landlord. In return for the managerial services, the investment group takes a portion of the rent, which becomes the source of its profits.

REITs,

A Real Estate Investment Trust works just like any publicly traded instrument. It works pretty much like trading and investing in the stock market. Stock market investors who want to include real estate properties in their portfolio can invest in REITs.

Final Word,

There are other types of investments that can be made in the world of real estate. Just like any other industry, there are profits that can be made and risks that need to be taken. There are other aspects about property investing that cannot be covered here but these might help new investors find the courage to take the plunge.

LEARNING ABOUT REAL ESTATE FRAUD AND WAYS TO AVOID THEM

Whatever kind of real estate market you may have right now, it will still be prone to various types of fraudulent activities. Con artists have perpetrated in the market, pretending to be the good people with their victims having less idea that they have malicious intent.

All sellers, buyers, and investors should learn to keep their guards up. It is possible for scam artists to take advantage of the situation, especially when there is a huge amount of money involved. And the sad part is, these people do not choose who they want to victimize. Whether you are financially stable or not, they can still trick you. If you are in a vulnerable state, you may be easily lured into their schemes.

Kinds of Real Estate Fraud,

As mentioned above, real estate fraud comes in different forms. Below are some of the examples:

1. In flipping properties, an investor can buy a property for less and end up selling the property for more than it's worth. Nothing is wrong within this, except there may be a possibility that documents and appraisal may be tampered to overstate the real value of the property.

2. A person trying to take over another person's property by pretending to be someone else. Hence, gaining rights of the property and then, disposing it for cash.

3. A lender allowing a borrower to overstate his or her assets and earnings so that they can grant the borrower a big amount of money for loan. In the end, the borrower becomes in the

losing end of rates and fees become too overwhelming for them.

These are just some of the instances where a fraud exists. Believe that there are still other forms of real estate fraud. Even people undergoing foreclosure can become a victim of it. It is a sad truth that there are people existing in exchange for the detriment of others.

However, the actions of other people can be beyond your control. The next best thing to do is to outsmart them.

Ways to Avoid Fraud,

Since real estate fraud can take form just about anything, you have to be ready for it. To help you out, below are some tips to apply to avoid becoming a victim of it:

1. If the parties offering to transact with you in exchange for profit or for money are people who you have never heard of, then you should doubt. If you seem interested in the whole business proposal, it is important that you do background checks to see if they are legal to run such business. You also have to check their business plans and strategy to know if it is feasible or not.

2. Never sign agreements or even wire money, unless you know exactly what you are getting yourself into. If there are things you do not understand, then better seek the help of a professional (a real estate agent or lawyer). As much as possible, find an independent party and do not go for people suggested by those offering an opportunity.

3. Transact with reputable financial institutions. If your lenders say it is okay to falsify documents, then you should take this as

your cue. From this alone, you can already tell how low the integrity of this people can be.

4. Never give out your personal information randomly. As much as possible, disclose it only to people, who you are sure to be legally doing business.

FACTS ABOUT REAL ESTATE BROKERAGES AND THEIR NON-PRODUCING LICENSED REAL ESTATE SALES PEOPLE

Ontario real estate Brokers who own and operate their own Brokerage Firm may have registered agents with them that are not active or non-producers, but these agents are still accumulating day to day expenses. They could be Brokers, Associate Brokers, or sales representatives, including real estate agent teams, and even husband and wife teams or partners alike.

There are many various reasons why agents come into the Brokerage business and then for good reason, do not become active in the day to day expected activities including sales that are expected from them. Some reasons may be as simple as agents having a change of heart due to disliking sales since it was not what they imagined it would be. Maybe an experience like having one of their own family members choose a real estate agent other than them to list and sell their house. Frustration like this is often severe enough to cause agents to quit the business.

Other reasons may be because of a change in their circumstances. Deciding to go part-time instead of full-time, pregnancy leave, another career opportunity, husband and wife teams where the wife is really a stay at home mom, taking time off due to sickness whether personal or family, already have a full-time job and their real estate license is really for future use, taking a sabbatical or 2 and deciding to back to school, etc. etc.

Most, if not all these reasons are valid enough to deter the agent from the high costs of operating. How could they avoid it though? If their Brokerage is a member of the local real estate board then each registered agent must be as well. This means high board fees and Association dues, like O.R.E.A. and C.R.E.A., aka, the Ontario Real Estate Association and the Canadian Real Estate Association. In addition, there may be franchise fees, "desk fees", monthly fees, advertising costs, stationary expenses and the like.

Real estate Brokers and Brokerages now have an option for these non-active, non-producing agents. A popular option is to refer these inactive agents to a real estate brokerage firm in Ontario that is not a member of any Ontario real estate board and who provide the service of accepting inactive agents as registrants in their Brokerage and holding their license. The Brokerage referring these agents to the latter are considered to be the Brokerage of Origin.

The Brokerage of Origin sometimes may benefit from such an arrangement since the agents being transferred may refer business back to them if the occasion ever arises. I addition, these transferring non-active agents have the option to return to the Brokerage of Origin if and when they decided to become active again. Therefore, the Broker Owners of these Ontario Realty Brokerages can now help by recommending their non-producing agents the option to "park their license", and save on unnecessary expenses.

Keeping their real estate license active and doing so at a much-reduced expense is the key here. These inactive agents can park their realty license and hold it active with a non-member Brokerage for a very low holding or parking fee but they must also inquire about some other issues beforehand. They should inquire about their share or commission split on referrals to other Brokerages and what the total expenses to park their license would be.

Non-active real estate agents in Ontario feel the financial pressure released as they decided to hold their license active by parking their license with a non-board member Brokerage. Their Brokerage of Origin also feels relieved and no longer have to concern themselves with unpaid expenses by their inactive agents.

REAL ESTATE INVESTING - REASONS TO INVEST IN REAL ESTATE NOW

There are some very good benefits to investing in real estate. First of all, there are tremendous tax advantages to owning properties. The ability to generate passive income is another benefit of owning houses. There is also a chance that your property will appreciate in value. These are just a few of the many reasons why people love to own houses. But there are also some disadvantages. It can take a lot of income, energy, time and effort to locate and rehab a property to get into move-in ready condition. This could be anywhere from a few weeks to a few months.

Once the property is in move-in condition then you have to find a tenant. If you're wholesaling properties, you have to make sure that there's enough spread to make it worth your time and effort. If you're doing lease options, you have to stay in the middle of the transaction until the buyer cashes you out. All of these different real estate techniques have their advantages, but they also have disadvantages.

Why does somebody by a drill? Is it because they want to own a drill? No, it's because they need a hole. The drill is the tool that they use to get the end result. In this example that would be a hole. Why do people buy real estate? Well, some people want to collect properties just like they collect other things. But the majority of people just want the benefits that real estate brings to them. They buy houses for the benefits, not just to buy real estate. The best real estate investment would be having the ability to enjoy the benefits of owning properties without getting your hands dirty or doing the heavy lifting that is involved in most real estate transactions.

That is the beauty of turnkey investing. Turnkey investing is when you buy a property that has already been rehabbed and is completely move-in ready and it usually has a tenant in it. The only thing the investor has to do is cash the checks each month. Everything else that was needed to be done to the property was done by somebody else. Now the investor can enjoy the benefits of owning real properties without dealing with the hassles of finding a property, rehabbing it and finding a tenant for it. Turnkey investing is really the best option for both new investors and experienced investors.

Instead of investing the time and resources into learning how to find the house and how to rehab it and how to find a tenant, the smart investors of today are outsourcing all the heavy lifting and going straight into enjoying the benefits of owning the property instead of looking for the property. They are leaving everything else to third-party experts who specialize in locating and fixing the properties. They simply buy these turnkey properties and add them to their portfolio. Whether you buy one or ten is completely up to you. Turnkey investing simply helps you get there much faster.

If you are a brand-new investor, this is a good way to get your feet wet without having to learn a bunch of techniques to buy properties. If you're an experienced pro, turnkey investing allows you to expand your portfolio without getting your hands dirty.

OTHER USEFUL TIPS ABOUT REAL ESTATE INVESTING

It can't be stressed enough that when you're starting out, don't rush to get the first piece of property that you see. It's important that you conduct your due diligence with everything regarding real estate investing.

Even though it is a lucrative and profitable business, you can also lose money if you don't work it properly. Don't listen to all of those stories that you hear about people making lots of money "overnight" with real estate investing. It takes more than a day to start seeing a profit. It can take more than a week to actually get a property that you want and can afford to get.

If you take your time and look around, you may be surprised as to how much is available to you in terms of real estate properties. There seems to never be a shortage of places where you can find a place to use for a profitable investment.

Once you get into real estate investing, it's important to stay in it for the long haul. That's the way you will create wealth. Regardless of whether the market is up or down, you must be willing to weather any storms that come about. There will be times when there are down markets, but you can't give up and throw in the towel.

It seems like those that are getting their feet wet want to get in when the iron is hot, but when it gets cold, they want to bail out. Gaining lucrative wealth from real estate investing comes with staying the course. Even in down times, you can still profit. There will always be people that are looking for a place to live.

You will be able to increase rent as time goes on. This will help you produce a surplus while you are still paying the same amount of your mortgage loan. This of course, can happen if you have a structured loan payment that doesn't fluctuate during any given period.

Getting into real estate investing can be a good experience for you. You would be learning one of the best ways to build up wealth.

Since you are not Superman, don't expect to do all of the repairs yourself. There may be some minor cosmetic issues you can take care of. Other than that, leave it up to the professionals. You don't want to get burned out before you get your feet wet.

It takes a lot to maintain and manage real estate properties. When you get to the point where you have a nice cash flow every month, you can hire a property management company to do the work for you. This will free you from the tasks that you would get used to doing yourself. That would include getting rental payments and dealing with various tenant issues.

When you do decide to purchase property for investing purposes, seek counsel from those who have come before you. It's important that you have adequate information before you jump into something like this. Real estate investing involves time and money. You need both in order to make this business work for you and you not working for it.

Find experienced investors that are willing to spend some time with you showing you some of the ins and outs of real estate investing. They can share some of their experiences with you and advise you on what to look out for. In addition to repairs, you will need to keep enough funds on hand in order to honor your mortgage loan obligations on time.

Having adequate knowledge prior to making that leap into a venture like this can help you avoid the pitfalls that can befall some new real estate investors. Getting into real estate investing can be exciting and lucrative, but you have to be willing to deal with the negatives as well as the positives.

Have realistic goals and remember that real estate investing is a process. Those who claimed to have gotten their wealth quickly through real estate investing probably don't have it now.

Most of all, try to keep an open mind and don't get yourself worked up when things go wrong, as they will when you have tenants. If you do your homework, you can avoid some of the issues that can happen to investors.

Getting the right tenant for your properties can sometimes be a hassle. However, it's better to take your time and get the right people so you can avoid a major headache later. You can get a sense of the kinds of people that would make good tenants.

They will have stability with their place of employment and have not hopped around like a rabbit, living in different places. Getting someone that has a good stability record is one of the main keys that can help you to get them as a tenant.

Another thing you need to think about is not trying to hoard a bunch of properties at once. Start out with one and then work your way up. Working at a slower pace will help you to properly maintain and manage what you have.

You will be successful once you employ strategies that take you from one step to the next. It's better to have properties that will provide you with a steady income than waiting on the next blockbuster that may take a while, meaning years to come. That's a negative cash flow scenario waiting to happen.

After you feel comfortable with the first one, then you may want to look for the next one, and so on. This will help you to appreciate your investments better as opposed to being in a hurry to make money and acquire wealth.

Be better than your competition. Don't just put up a sign and hope that people will come. You have to market and advertise. You may need to place ads in the paper and get with seasoned real estate professionals to help you.

Not everyone you ask will be willing to step up to the plate, but you will find a few that won't mind spending the time to help you along the way. Of course, you still have to conduct your due diligence.

Eventually, you will have so many investment properties, you won't have a choice but to hire a property management company to take over. Of course, you will have to set aside funds to pay them for their services. That's all the more reason for you to take it easy when it comes to building wealth with real estate investments.

Before you know it, you'll be on your way to building wealth with real estate investment properties.

ADVANTAGES AND DISADVANTAGES OF REAL ESTATE INVESTING

Investing in real estate can bring a large cash flow for many investors, but only if they invest in the right properties. Investors who are new to investing should not invest in the land right away because the investment of land is considered a drain on cash. The real money is in large commercial properties and flipping houses. In order to stay successful in property investing, a person should only concentrate in one area. If a person is investing in commercial property, they should only stick to those areas, instead of crossing over to investing in homes. Trying to do both at the same time can create more of a loss in investments, and can be draining and time-consuming. Investing in real estate takes a lot of experience, knowledge, and contacts. Starting out small is always best for real estate investors so that they can learn the ropes, and make contacts while in the process. In the investment world, one contact always leads to another. There are more advantages to investing in property than there are disadvantages. The disadvantages of investing is that everything is always a gamble. Just as investing in the stock market is a gamble, so it is with property investing. That is why it is so important that investors invest their money in the right properties that will be sure to bring a profit.

When investing in conventional property, flipping houses is always a sure bet that an investor will not lose their shirts. Whether a flipped house sales successfully or not, does not mean that an investor will lose out on their money. They always have the advantage of renting out their homes until they find adequate buyers, or until the real estate market starts to boom again. It is also important for real estate investors to know when it is a buyers market or a seller's market when trying to get the most out of their investments. Flipping houses can be a real advantage when an investor can make large profits from flipping a house, and then selling it for a larger profit. Investing in commercial real estate is also an advantage because large commercial investments can bring a large monthly income. There is also a lot of competition in the investment world. Understanding marketing strategies are crucial when it comes to competition.

Another advantage for real estate investing is to be pre-qualified by banks and lenders before people start investing. This will give them a bigger advantage over investors who have not pre-qualified yet. Businesses and home owners are more willing to sell their property to an investor who has already been approved to buy the property.

CONCLUSION

We've covered quite a few points throughout this tutorial. Below are some of the main points that were made along the way:

• Real estate investments fall into one of the four following categories: private equity, public equity, private debt and public debt. Your choice of which one to invest in depends on the type of exposure you are seeking for your portfolio.

• You can invest in either income-producing properties or non-income-producing properties. Any leased property is income producing, and vacant properties are non-income producing. You can still earn a capital return on a non-income producing property, just as you would on an investment in a home.

• The major types of investment properties are offices, retails, industrials and multi-family residential properties.

• Real estate can produce income (like a bond) and appreciate (like an equity).

• Real estate is tangible, so it requires ongoing management. On the other hand, you also have an increased ability to influence the performance of a single investment as compared to other asset classes.

• Some of the benefits of adding real estate to a portfolio include diversification, yield enhancement, risk reduction and inflation-hedging capabilities. However, real estate also has high transaction costs, can be difficult to acquire and it is challenging to measure its relative performance.

• Buying real estate requires substantial due diligence to ensure that you're getting what you expect after you close.

• The way to determine the value of your property (other than actually selling it) is to have it appraised by an accredited appraiser.

If you enjoyed this book and found it useful, please leave a review on Amazon

I would really appreciate that, your support really does make a difference and I read all the reviews personally so I can get your feedback and make this book even better.

Thanks again for your support!

www.ingramcontent.com/pod-product-compliance
Lightning Source LLC
Chambersburg PA
CBHW051238170526
45165CB00004B/1488